Kaladhar DSVGK, M. A. Prasad, S Sri Krishna Keerthi

Ayurmedbase. An Ayurvedic Medicinal Database for Traditional and Ayurvedic Medicinal Systems

GRIN Verlag

Bibliografische Information der Deutschen Nationalbibliothek:

Die Deutsche Bibliothek verzeichnet diese Publikation in der Deutschen National-bibliografie; detaillierte bibliografische Daten sind im Internet über http://dnb.d-nb.de/ abrufbar.

Impressum:

Copyright © 2014 GRIN Verlag GmbH
Druck und Bindung: Books on Demand GmbH, Norderstedt Germany
ISBN: 978-3-656-73965-4

Dieses Buch bei GRIN:

http://www.grin.com/de/e-book/280031/ayurmedbase-an-ayurvedic-medicinal-database-for-traditional-and-ayurvedic

GRIN - Your knowledge has value

Der GRIN Verlag publiziert seit 1998 wissenschaftliche Arbeiten von Studenten, Hochschullehrern und anderen Akademikern als eBook und gedrucktes Buch. Die Verlagswebsite www.grin.com ist die ideale Plattform zur Veröffentlichung von Hausarbeiten, Abschlussarbeiten, wissenschaftlichen Aufsätzen, Dissertationen und Fachbüchern.

Besuchen Sie uns im Internet:

http://www.grin.com/

http://www.facebook.com/grincom

http://www.twitter.com/grin_com

Ayurmedbase: An Ayurvedic Medicinal Database for Traditional and Ayurvedic Medicinal Systems

DOWLURU S V G K KALADHAR
Mr. M.A.Prasad
S Sri Krishna Keerthi

Table of Contents

CHAPTER 1

INTRODUCTION

1.1 Background

Four thousand years ago the medical knowledge of Indian sub continent was termed as ayurveda. Ayurveda remains an important system of medicine and drug therapy in India. In India, around 20,000 medicinal and herbal plants have been recorded. Hardly 7000 plants are being used for curing different diseases. Many of the pharmaceutical industries depend on these plant products.

Plant derived medicines have been the first line of defense in maintaining health and combating diseases. According to a WHO estimate, about 80% of the world population relies on traditional systems of medicines for primary health care, where plants form the dominant component over other resources [1].

Chemical principles from natural sources have become much simpler and have contributed to the development of new drugs from medicinal plants. The degradation of natural resources i.e. herbal products is a major threat to medicinal plants in India [2]. There are various plant species in medicinal use which we come across in our daily life, and few of them with unknown usage. Scientists from past knew a lot about these plants and their importance.

1.2 Objectives

A medicinal herb is different from botanical term "herb". It refers to any plants used for medicinal purposes. For example, a medicinal herb can be a real herbal plant, a shrub, other woody plant, or a fungus. Commonly used parts are seeds, berries, leaves, barks, roots, fruits, or a mushroom, which may be considered as "herbs" in medicinal use. Many of the modern medicines are produced indirectly from medicinal plants. Plants are directly used as medicines by a majority of cultures around the world, for example Indian medicine and Chinese medicine. Many food crops have medicinal effects, for example garlic.

1

In this concern, a database has been designed for medicinal/ herbal plants with the following objectives:

1. Collection of medicinal data.
2. Web designing for medicinal plants using HTML/SQL/PHP.
3. Screening of medicinal plants based on diseases
4. Screening based on family.
5. Screening of herbs based on their vernacular names.

1.3 Purpose, Scope and Applicability

1.3.1 Purpose

The most appropriate way to gain knowledge about them and their usage can be resolved by creating a database from the publications in Ayurveda, papers and books on botany. A database on medicinal plants and their treatment of different disorders with clear linkage of each species is included along with the information about all the medicinal plants and herbs found in and around Andhra Pradesh with their scientific names, common names, pictures and their therapeutic properties, selection of these herbs as a medicine etc.

1.3.2 Scope

The aim of the present research is to understand the knowledge of plants used in medicines, to preserve this traditional heritage, to rationalize the usage and can easily identify the rare and extinct plants for the conservation.

1.3.3 Applicability

The main application is to fine medicinal plant/any data in the database. The following are the tools used in the present application.

1.3.3.1 SQL

SQL is a tool for organizing, managing, and retrieving data stored by a computer database. The acronym SQL is an abbreviation for *Structured Query Language*. For historical reasons, SQL is usually pronounced "sequel," but the alternate pronunciation "S.Q.L." is also used. As the name implies, SQL is a computer *language* that you use to interact with a database. In fact, SQL works with one specific type of database, called a *relational database*.

2

The name Structured Query Language is actually somewhat of a misnomer. First of all, SQL is far more than a query tool, although that was its original purpose, and retrieving data is still one of its most important functions.

SQL is used to control all of the functions that a DBMS provides for its users, including:

• **Data definition.** SQL lets a user define the structure and organization of the stored data and relationships among the stored data items.

• **Data retrieval.** SQL allows a user or an application program to retrieve stored data from the database and use it.

• **Data manipulation.** SQL allows a user or an application program to update the database by adding new data, removing old data, and modifying previously stored data.

• **Access control.** SQL can be used to restrict a user's ability to retrieve, add, and modify data, protecting stored data against unauthorized access.

• **Data sharing.** SQL is used to coordinate data sharing by concurrent users, ensuring that they do not interfere with one another.

• **Data integrity.** SQL defines integrity constraints in the database, protecting it from corruption due to inconsistent updates or system failures.

• SQL is a *client/server language.* Personal computer programs use SQL to communicate over a network with database servers that store shared data. This client/server architecture has become very popular for enterprise-class applications.

• SQL is an *Internet data access language*. Internet web servers that interact with corporate data and Internet applications servers all use SQL as a standard language for accessing corporate databases.

SQL is thus a comprehensive language for controlling and interacting with a database management system.

1.3.3.2 HTML

HTML stands for **H**yper **T**ext **M**arkup **L**anguage. HTML is a language for describing web pages.

HTML is not a programming language, it is a **markup language.** A markup language is a set of **markup tags.** HTML uses **markup tags** to describe web pages

Creating an HTML document is easy. To begin coding we just need a simple text editor.

HTML has not been around for many years. November 1990 marks the day of the first web page and back then there were little to no HTML standards to be followed. A group called the World Wide Web Consortium was then formed and have since set the standards that are widely accepted

Tag - Used to specify ("mark-up") regions of HTML documents for the web browser to interpret. Tags look like this: <tag>

Element - A complete tag, having an opening <tag> and a closing </tag>.

Attribute - Used to modify the value of the HTML element. Elements will often have multiple attributes. HTML documents **contain HTML tags** and plain text
HTML markup tags are usually called HTML tags
- HTML tags are keywords surrounded by **angle brackets** like <html>
- HTML tags normally **come in pairs** like <b> and </b>
- The first tag in a pair is the **start tag,** the second tag is the **end tag**
- Start and end tags are also called **opening tags** and **closing tags**
-

Web pages have many uses. Here are some important facts about why web pages are so useful.

4

- A cheap and easy way to spread information to a large audience.
- Another medium to market your business.
- To know about personal details.

1.3.3.3 PHP

PHP stands for PHP Hypertext Preprocessor.

PHP is an HTML-embedded scripting language. Much of its syntax is borrowed from C, Java and Perl with a couple of unique PHP-specific features thrown in. The goal of the language is to allow web developers to write dynamically generated pages quickly."Another way to think of PHP is a powerful, behind the scenes scripting language that your visitors won't see!

When someone visits PHP webpage, the web server processes the PHP code. It then sees which parts it needs to show to visitors(content and pictures) and hides the other stuff , then translates your PHP into HTML. After the translation into HTML, it sends the webpage to the visitor's web browser.

PHP will allow to: Reduce the time to create large websites and Creates a customized user experience for visitors based on information that you have gathered from them.

1.3.3.4 WAMP SERVER

For the creation of a database all that we need is a platform to work on SQL, HTML and PHP. One such platform to build and run websites in offline mode is **WampServer.** This Wamp server's functions can manage our MySQL and PHP services. WampServer is a Windows web development environment. It allows us to create web applications with not only PHP and a MySQL database, but also with Apache 2. PHPMyAdmin is a feature of wamp, where we can create our sql tables. This database can be further linked up with the PHP code and can be displayed as the webpage with our query retrieved.

1.4 Achievements

The main achievement is to construct the medicinal plant data that is useful for the human community.

1.5 Organization of report

The project work contains following chapters

1. Introduction
2. Survey of technologies
3. Requireents and analysis
4. System design
5. Implementation and testing
6. Results and discussion
7. Conclusion

CHAPTER 2

SURVEY OF TECHNOLOGIES

Asia is the largest continent and has 60% of the world's population. It has abundant medicinal and aromatic plant species, well documented traditional knowledge, a long-standing practice of traditional medicine, and the potential for social and economic development of medicinal and aromatic plants (MAPs). Asia is one of the largest biodiversity regions in the world, containing some of the richest countries in plant resources. The continent has diverse plant flora but species richness is concentrated mainly in tropical and subtropical regions. Six of the world's 18 biodiversity hot spots, namely eastern Himalaya, North Borneo, Peninsular Malaysia, Sri Lanka, Philippines and the Western Ghats of South India, lie in Asia [3].

The study of medicinal plants is being revived again. Although they have been used for millennia by tribal and ethnic communities throughout the world, only in recent years medicinal plants have attracted global interest as they constitute a rich treasure trove of cultural information and are sources of natural products, which provide health security to millions in rural communities. In recent years there has been renewed interest in natural medicines that are obtained from plant parts or plant extracts. Nearly 40 percent or more of the pharmaceuticals currently used in western countries are derived or at least partially derived from natural sources [4]. Medicinal plants are considered as source of various alkaloids and other chemical substances essential for mankind [5].

Medicinal plants used to treat hypoglycemic or hyperglycemic conditions are of considerable interest for ethno-botanical community as they are recognized to contain valuable medicinal properties in different parts of the plant and a number of plants have shown varying degree of hypoglycemic and anti-hyperglycemic activity [6]. The hypoglycemic effect of several plants used as anti-diabetic remedies has been confirmed, and the mechanisms of hypoglycemic activity of these plants are being studied [7].

The treatment of diabetes with synthetic drugs is generally not preferred because of its high cost and the range of side effects caused. Hence development of traditional or alternative

7

medicine is needed. Herbal drugs constitute an important part of traditional medicine and literature shows that there are more than 400 plant species showing anti-diabetic activity [8]. In most part of the world, the information on medicinal plants has generally been handed down from generation to generation only by means of folklore, which may disappear over a period of time. For effective conservation of phyto-diversity and the successful documentation of medicinal plants, the systematic inventory of medicinal plants is necessary.

The relevant data (detailed description of medicinal herbs, therapeutic uses) on such plants in organized and easy to understand format, with illustrations, is available in the database. The integrated database with interactive analytical and visualization tools, having multiple editing options, allows users to investigate many questions without requiring time-consuming inferences from the literature or multiple data sets. The activity prediction for phyto-chemicals forms an important part of the work. The NeMedPlant database would be useful for prediction of activities of natural as well as synthetic products and identifying drug leads having low toxicity and high bioavailability [9].

Medicinal plants documented in the literature from thick vegetations of the world are routinely used for high throughput screening in small molecular drug discovery. A large number of such plants are known to be recognized in a discrete manner. Therefore, it is important to store information related to medicinal and aromatic plants of JK in a database. This will help in the use and exploitation of the plant materials for drug discovery. Some of the plants available in this region are also known to have aromatic value. Here, we describe the development and use of a database containing information on medicinal and aromatic plants from Jammu Kashmir [10].

The Floral Reflectance Database (FReD) has been developed to make an extensive collection of spectral reflectance data for flower species collected from all over the world available to researchers. These could, for example, be used in modelling interactions between pollinator vision and plant signals, or analyses of flower colors' in various habitats. The database contains functions for calculating flower colour loci according to widely-used models of bee colour space, reflectance graphs of the spectra and an option to search for flowers with similar colors' in bee colour space[11].

Herbal drug development includes various steps, starting from a passport data on raw materials, correct identification, pharmacognostic and chemical quality standardization, safety and preclinical pharmacology, clinical pharmacology and randomized, controlled clinical trials. Addressing standardization is vital and needs broader consideration. Ayurvedic medicine was developed at times of limited access to technologically variable norms of standardization. The dynamic process of evolution could alter and affect the identity and structure of natural materials. For commercialization, correct identification and supply of raw material to avoid adulteration has become a challenge.

Additionally, some botanical species might have been extinct. Lastly, the properties of botanicals as recorded in classics may have undergone change due to time and environmental factors. Standardization of ayurvedic botanicals and medicines is required, although one cannot readily apply the typical modern pharmaceutical pharmacopoeial standards. The concept of active markers in the process of standardization needs a flexible approach in favour of the complex nature of these materials [12].

The basis of human personality as given in ancient Hindu Ayurvedan literature is reviewed and interpreted in the light of current knowledge and understanding. The structure of mind expounded in *Sankhyan* philosophy is explained and its parallelism with the Freudian approach is brought out. The formative influences in the development of the mental constitution of an individual are described. An attempt is made to demonstrate close similarity between Ayurvedan and Lewin's field (Gestalt) theories. Significance of Tridosh (*Vat, Pitta* and *Kaf*), by vitiating the chemical balance, as estiological factors of mental illness is described. Sixteen presonality types and their correspondence with 16 types of mental disorders are mentioned [13].

'Impeding crude drug research, no less than performing it, has ethical consequences. Not to act is to act.' As long as no serious attempt is made to develop appropriate methods for assessing the therapeutic actions of whole medicinal plants and of preparations made from them, any refusal to accept them as therapeutic agents may be regarded as unscientific. This attitude also goes against the highest dictum of medical practice - *Salus aegroti suprema lex.* I t deprives the Physician of existing means for helping mankind [14].

9

HerbMed - an interactive, electronic herbal database - provides hyperlinked access to the scientific data underlying the use of herbs for health. This public site provides free access to 20 of the most popular herbs. Most herbal resources on the World Wide Web provide summaries of the data that have been interpreted and presented from a particular point of view. HerbMed provides "as is", neutral access to the data underlying the medicinal use of herbs. HerbMed also provides uniquely comprehensive access to the available scientific publications and data on each herb, with dynamic updating to ensure completeness [15].

PlantCARE is a database of plant *cis*-acting regulatory elements, enhancers and repressors. Regulatory elements are represented by positional matrices, consensus sequences and individual sites on particular promoter sequences. Data about the transcription sites are extracted mainly from the literature, supplemented with an increasing number of *in silico* predicted data. Apart from a general description for specific transcription factor sites, levels of confidence for the experimental evidence, functional information and the position on the promoter are given. [16].

CHAPTER 3

REQUIREMENTS AND ANALYSIS

The project work design and development requires following tools/ interfaces

1. PHP
2. MySQL
3. Web Browser
4. Client

   System configuration like Intel (R), Pentium(R) 4 CPU 3.00 GHz, 504MB of RAM, Microsoft Windows XP OS

5. Server

   System configuration like Intel (R), Pentium(R) 4 CPU 3.00 GHz, 504MB of RAM, Microsoft Windows XP OS

CHAPTER 4

SYSTEM DESIGN

4.1 Modules

4.1.1 Database Interface

The interface is designed for searching the dataset using a PHP (a programming language that allows web developers to create dynamic content that interacts with databases) server enabled script for keywords such as botanical name, local name, family, medicinal use [17,18].

4.1.2 Database Design

The database is developed in MySQL on a Windows Platform and can be updated regularly.

4.2 Data design

Data is collected from various sources and was designed based on procedural coding.

Tables are the basic unit of data storage in any database.Data is stored in **rows** and **columns**. We must define a table with a **table name** and set of columns. Give each column a **column name** , a **datatype** (such as VARCHAR2, INT), and a **width**. The width can be predetermined by the datatype, as in DATE. A row is a collection of column information corresponding to a single record. You can specify rules for each column of a table. These rules are called **integrity constraints**. One example is a NOT NULL integrity constraint. This constraint forces the column to contain a value in every row. After you create a table, insert rows of data using SQL statements. Table data can then be queried, deleted, or updated using SQL.

SQL can be divided into two parts: The Data Manipulation Language (DML) and the Data Definition Language(DDL).
The query and update commands form the DML part of SQL:

• **SELECT** - extracts data from a database
• **UPDATE** - updates data in a database
• **DELETE** - deletes data from a database
• **INSERT INTO** - inserts new data into a database

The DDL part of SQL permits database tables to be created or deleted. It also defines indexes (keys), specify links between tables, and impose constraints between tables. The most important DDL statements in SQL are:
• **CREATE DATABASE** - creates a new database
• **ALTER DATABASE** - modifies a database
• **CREATE TABLE** - creates a new table
• **ALTER TABLE** - modifies a table
• **DROP TABLE** - deletes a table

- **CREATE INDEX** - creates an index (search key)
- **DROP INDEX** - deletes an index

Syntax

SQL CREATE DATABASE Syntax

CREATE DATABASE database_name

SQL CREATE TABLE Syntax
CREATE TABLE table_name
(
column_name1 data_type,
column_name2 data_type,
column_name3 data_type,....)

SQL INSERT INTO Syntax
INSERT INTO table_name (column1, column2, column3,...)
VALUES (value1, value2, value3,...)
Or INSERT INTO table_name VALUES (value1, value2, value3,...)

SQL UPDATE Syntax
UPDATE table_name
SET column1=value, column2=value2,...
WHERE some_column=some_value

SQL DELETE Syntax
DELETE FROM table_name
WHERE some_column=some_value

SQL SELECT Syntax
SELECT column_name(s)
FROM table_name

Or SELECT * FROM table_name

SQL ALTER TABLE Syntax

ALTER TABLE table_name
ADD column_name datatype

ALTER TABLE table_name
DROP COLUMN column_name

ALTER TABLE table_name
ALTER COLUMN column_name datatype

4.3 Codes

4.3.1 MySQL
Create database database

Table common_name

Create table common_name (sno int[80], scientific_name varchar[45], common_name varchar[45], telugu_name varchar[45], family varchar[45])

INSERT INTO `common_names`(`scientific_name`, `common_name`, `telugu_name`, `family`, `sno`) VALUES ([value-1],[value-2],[value-3],[value-4],[value-5])

Values are entered into the table common_names in the following format

INSERT INTO `common_names`(`sno`,`scientific_name`, `common_name`, `telugu_name`, `family`,) VALUES (1, *'Abrus precatorius'*, 'Indian Liquorice', 'Gurivinda theega , Guri ginja', 'Fabaceae'),

(2, *'Abutilon indicum* (Linn) sweet.', 'Country Mallow', 'Duvvena chettu, Tuthari benda, Mudra benda', 'Malvaceae'),

(3, *'Acacia arabica* willd.', 'Black babool, Indian Gum Arabic tree', 'Nalla tumma', 'Mimosaceae'),

(4, *'Acalypha indica* Linn', 'Indian acalypha', 'Moorkonda, kuppinta', 'Euphorbiaceae'),

(5, *'Achyranthus aspera* Linn', 'Prickly flower', 'Uttareni', 'Amaranthaceae'),

.
.// matter deleted to save space
.
.(147 , *'Zingiber officinale roscoe'*, 'Ginger, Dried ginger', 'Allam - sonti', 'Zingiberaceae');

Table diseases

INSERT INTO `diseases`(`disease_no`, `disease`, `herbal_species`) VALUES ([value-1],[value-2],[value-3])

Values are inserted into diseases table

INSERT INTO `diseases`(`disease_no`, `disease`, `herbal_species`) VALUES (1,'Abdominal Pain/worms','Abrus precatorius'),

(2,'Abdominal Pain/worms',*'Acalypha indica Linn'*),

14

(3,'Abdominal Pain/worms',*'Acoras calamus'*),

(4,'Abdominal Pain/worms',*'Aristolochia bracteolata Lamk'*),

(5,'Abdominal Pain/worms',*'Azardirachta indica A.Juss.'*),

(6,'Abdominal Pain/worms',*'Butea monosperma (Limk.) Taub.'*),

(7,'Abdominal Pain/worms',*'Carica papaya (Linn.)'*),

(8,'Abdominal Pain/worms',*'Casealpinia bonduc (Linn).Roxb'*),

(9,'Abdominal Pain/worms',*'Cinnamomum aromaticum'*),

(10,'Abdominal Pain/worms',*'Clitoria ternatea Linn'*),

.

.

.//// matter deleted to save space

.

.

.

(515,'Wounds',*'Mimosa catechu & Acacia catechu'*),

(516,'Wounds',*'Musa paradisiaca Linn.'*),

(517,'Wounds',*'Nicotiana tobacum'*),

(518,'Wounds',*'Tephrosia purpurea (Linn). Pers.'*);

4.3.2 HTML Syntax

```
<HTML>
        <head>
             <title>
             </title>
        </head>
    <body>
    </body>
</HTML>
```

A html code starts with the <HTML> and ends with the off tag </HTML>

All the text processing, image processing tags are included inside the <body>.

<img>..........</img> - Image tag

................</br> - line break tag

<p>.................</p> - paragraph tag

<font>...............</font>- font tag

<marquee>........</marquee>- scroll tag

<blockquote>........</blockquote>- indent tag

<a href="url/path">...........</a> - anchor tag/ hyperlink tag

 In few tags, we can give different attributes:

Height , width, background, bgcolor, align, size. etc.,

HTML Codes

//for frames on the main page- main.html

<html>

<frameset rows="25%,75%" bordercolor="black">

 <frame src="search.html" />

<frameset cols="25,75">

<frame src="links.html"/>

 <frame src="home.html" name="x"/> </frameset></frameset></html>

//for links on the left frame – links.html

<html>

<body background=" brightgreen.jpg">

<center><font face="pristina" color="black" size=12><b>Overview:</font></b></center>

<center><font face="pristina" size=6><a style="color:black" href="home.html"
target="x">HOME</a> </p></font></center>

16

```
<center><font face="pristina" size=6><a style="color:black"  href="alphabets.html" target
="x">HERBS LIST</a></p> </font></center>

<center><font face="pristina" size=6><a style="color:black"  href="diseaselist.html" target
="x">PHYTO MEDICINE</a> </p></font></center>

<center><font face="pristina" size=6><a style="color:black"  href="family.php" target
="x">FAMILIES</a> </p></font></center>

<center><font face="pristina" size=6><a style="color:black"  href="teluguname.php" target
="x">TELUGU NAMES</a> </p></font></center>

</html>

</body>
```

// **home.html**

```html
<html>
<body background="xin.jpg">
<h1><b>HOME:</b></h1>
<font face="gabriola" color="black" size="6" align="center">
    India has been known to be rich repository of medicinal plants...............
This promotes the importance of ayurveda and focuses on conservation of therapeutically
important herbs.
</font>
</body>
</html>
```

//**alphabetically arranged herbs- alphabets.html**

```html
<html>
<body  background ="green.jpg"  text=black align=center>

<h1>Browse the herbs alphabetically</h1>
  <div class="alphabet_blockf" align="middle">
<font face="gabriola" size="12">

 <a  style="color:black" href="a.html" class="currentAlphabetf"> A</a>
<a style="color:black" href="b.html" > B</a>
<a style="color:black" href="c.html" > C</a>
<a  style="color:black" href="d.html" > D</a>
.
.
.

// matter deleted to save space
.
.
.

<a style="color:black" href="w.html" > W</a>
<a style="color:black" href="x.html" > X</a>
<a style="color:black" href="y.html" > Y</a>
            <a style="color:black"href="z.html" > Z</a><br>
  </font>
<font face="gabriola" size="6" color="black"> Andhra Pradesh is a treasure house of a wide
variety of medicinal plants. Few are found wild, while a number of species are being
domesticated by the farmers. ,most of the species are being grown in homesteads and are
becoming a part of traditional home remedies.<br>
Important medicinal plants are displayed here with their distribution, and therapeutic
activities </font></div>
</body></html>
```

//**code for a medicinal plant – Hibiscus rosa - sinensis Linn..html**

```html
<html>
<body text="black"><h1>Hibiscus</h1><br>
```

18

<font size=4><strong>Botanical Name</strong> – <i><b>Hibiscus rosa - sinensis
Linn.</b></i>
<b>English</b> – Hibiscus, Shoe flower
<b>Hindi</b> –Mandara, Japa
<b>Telugu</b> -Mandaram
<b>Family</b> – Malvaceae

<b>Description:</b>
<p align="justify">
Hibiscus is a flowering plant growing up to 8 meters with branches and sub branches.
Flowers are red usually called as Mudhamandaram or Rekamandaram, By sowing a stem
into the soil, it grows as a tree.

<b>Uses:</b>
<p align="justify">
1. Flowers 2-3 are fried in ghee and by eating these flowers along with that ghee well control
Menorrhagia.

 </font><div id="extras">
<img width="300" height="300"
src="MANDARAM.jpg" alt="" />   </img> </div> <h2 align= "right"><a
style="color:black" href="a.html"><b><i>Back</b></i></a></h2></body></html>

In the same way all the 147 html pages were created for the medicinal plants.

// code displaying diseases in clickable buttons: <u>diseaselist.html</u>

```
<html>
<body background="rofl.jpg" text=black>
<h2 align="center">Click on the disease button</h2><form>

 <marquee background=" " align="right" behavior="scroll" direction="left" scrollamount="5"
onMouseover="this.scrollAmount=0" onMouseout="this.scrollAmount=5">

<img src="stomach.jpg" width="100" height="100" alt="" />   
<img src="skin.jpg" width="100" height="100" alt="" />   
<img src="vomit.jpg" width="100" height="100" alt="" />
</marquee>
<blockquote> <p> A</P>
<a href="displaydisease.php?disease=Abdominal pain/worms" ><input type="button"
value="Abdominal pain/worms"></a></p>
<a href="displaydisease.php?disease=Allergy"><input type="button" value="Allergy"></a>
<a href="displaydisease.php?disease=Asthma"><input type="button" value="Asthma"></a>
 <P> B</P>
<a href="displaydisease.php?disease=Back pain"><input type="button"
value="Backpain"></a>
<a href="displaydisease.php?disease=Baldness"><input type="button"
value="Baldness"></a>
//c---------z//
<blockquote></form></body></html>
```

PHP Syntax
A PHP script always starts with **<?php** and ends with **?>**. A PHP script can be placed
anywhere in the document. A PHP file must have a .php extension. A PHP file normally
contains HTML tags, and some PHP scripting code. There are two basic statements to output
text with PHP: **echo** and **print**.

4.3.3 Simple php displaying hello as output

```php
<?php
$myString="Hello";
echo$myString;
?>
```

Connection to our Database

```php
<?
mysql_connect("mysql.yourhost.com","user_name","password") or die(mysql_error());
mysql_select_db("database_name") or die(mysql_error());

?>
```

We display the results

```php
while($result = mysql_fetch_array( $data ))
 {
echo $result['fname'];
echo " ";
}
```

Php to display result in table

```php
<tr>
<td><?php echo $row['table']; ?></td>
<td><a href="<?php echo $row['column_name']; ?>.html"><?php echo
$row['column_name']; ?></a></td>
</tr>
```

PHP-linkage to SQL
// code displaying herbs list when clicked on the disease button: <u>displaydisease.php</u>

```php
<html>
<body background="gr.jpg">
<table align="center" cellspacing="5" cellpadding="5" border="5" bordercolor="black">
<tr>
<td><b>DISEASE</b></td>
<td><b>HERBAL SPECIES</b></td>
</tr>

<?php
$disease=$_GET['disease'];
$con=mysql_connect("localhost","root","") or die(mysql_error());
mysql_select_db("database") or die(mysql_error());
$query="select * from diseases where disease='$disease'";
```

20

```php
$result=mysql_query($query);
$i=1;
while($row=mysql_fetch_array($result))
{
?>

<tr>
<td><?php echo $row['disease']; ?></td>
<td><a style="color:black" href="<?php echo $row['herbal_species']; ?>.html"><?php echo
$row['herbal_species']; ?></a></td>
</tr>

<?php
$i++;
}
?>
</table>
</body>
</html>
```

//program for "search" inside the database

```php
<html>
<body>

<?php

 mysql_connect("localhost","root","") or die(mysql_error());
 mysql_select_db("database") or die(mysql_error());


 $keyword = mysql_real_escape_string($_POST['keyword']);


 $query = "SELECT * FROM diseases WHERE MATCH(disease,herbal_species)
AGAINST ('$keyword')";

 $result = mysql_query($query);

  if (mysql_num_rows($result) > 0) {

  printf("Results: <br />");

  while ($row = mysql_fetch_array($result)) {

    printf("Result %s: <a href='displaycode.php?id=%s'>%s</a>",
           $row['disease'], $row['herbal_species'],ucfirst($row['herbal_species']));

  }

 } else {
  printf("No results found");
 }

?>

</body></html>
```

// **Displaying table with Scientific names, common names, families as columns.**
Connection between SQL table and the HTML pages: <u>family.php</u>

```
<html>
<body background="flux.jpg">
 
<font face="gabriola" align="center"><h1><b>LIST OF FAMILIES AND COMMON
NAMES</b><h1></font>
<table background="gr.jpg" align="center" cellpadding="5" cellspacing="5" border="5"
bordercolor="black">
<tr>
<td ><b>SCIENTIFIC NAME</b></td>
<td ><b>COMMON NAME</b></td>
<td ><b>FAMILY</b></td>
</tr>
<?php
$con=mysql_connect("localhost","root","") or die(mysql_error());
mysql_select_db("database") or die(mysql_error());
$query="select scientific_name,common_name,family from common_names";
$result=mysql_query($query);
$i=1;
while($row=mysql_fetch_array($result))
{
?>
<tr>
<td ><a style="color:black" href="<?php echo $row['scientific_name']; ?>.html"><?php echo
$row['scientific_name']; ?></a></td>
<td ><?php echo $row['common_name']; ?></td>
<td ><?php echo $row['family']; ?></td>
</tr>
<?php
}

?>
</body>
</html>
```

23

// **Connection between SQL and HTML through PHP displaying the columns- scientific names, common names and telugu names: teluguname.php**

```
<html>
<body background="flux.jpg">
 
<font face="gabriola" align="center"><h1><b>LIST OF TELUGU NAMES AND
COMMON NAMES</b><h1></font>
<table background="gr.jpg" align="center" cellpadding="5" cellspacing="5" border="5"
bordercolor="black">
<tr>
<td ><b>SCIENTIFIC NAMES</b></td>
<td ><b>COMMON NAMES</b></td>
<td ><b>TELUGU NAMES</b></td>
</tr>
<?php
$con=mysql_connect("localhost","root","") or die(mysql_error());
mysql_select_db("database") or die(mysql_error());
$query="select scientific_name,common_name,telugu_name from common_names";
$i=1;
$result=mysql_query($query);
while($row=mysql_fetch_array($result))
{
?>
<tr>
<td><a style="color:black" href="<?php echo $row['scientific_name']; ?>.html"><?php echo
$row['scientific_name']; ?></a></td>
<td ><?php echo $row['common_name']; ?></td>
<td ><?php echo $row['telugu_name']; ?></td>

</tr>
<?php
}

?>
</body>
</html>
```

24

CHAPTER 5

IMPLEMENTATION AND TESTING

SQL CODING is done through WAMP SERVER'S phpMyAdmin where a database with the name **DATABASE** and tables with the names **common_names** and **diseases** were created.[Fig1]

Fig 1: Creation of tables in phpMyAdmin

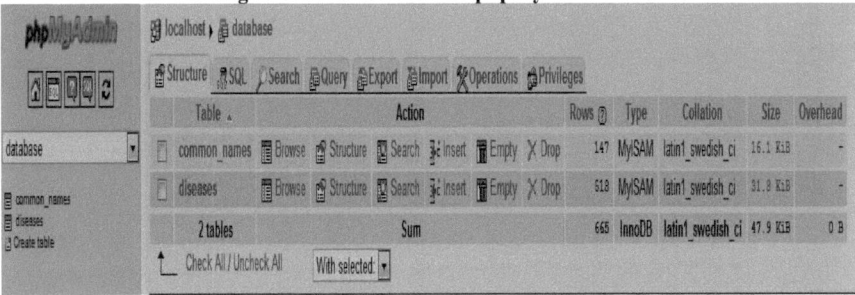

Table common_names includes the following information: Scientific_name, common_name, telugu_name, family set as the column names. Details of the medicinal plants are inserted into the rows. 147 rows have been inserted into this table. [Fig 2]

Fig 2: Common_names table in phpMyAdmin

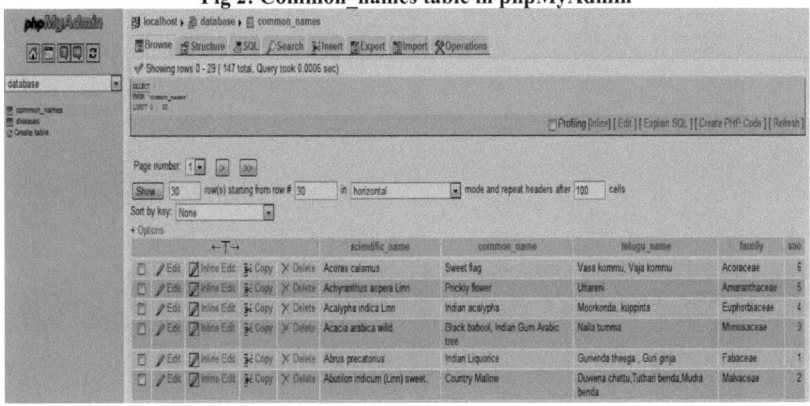

Table diseases consist of list of diseases with their related herbal_species as the column name.
518 rows were inserted into the diseases table. [Fig 3]

25

Fig 3: Disease table in phpMyAdmin

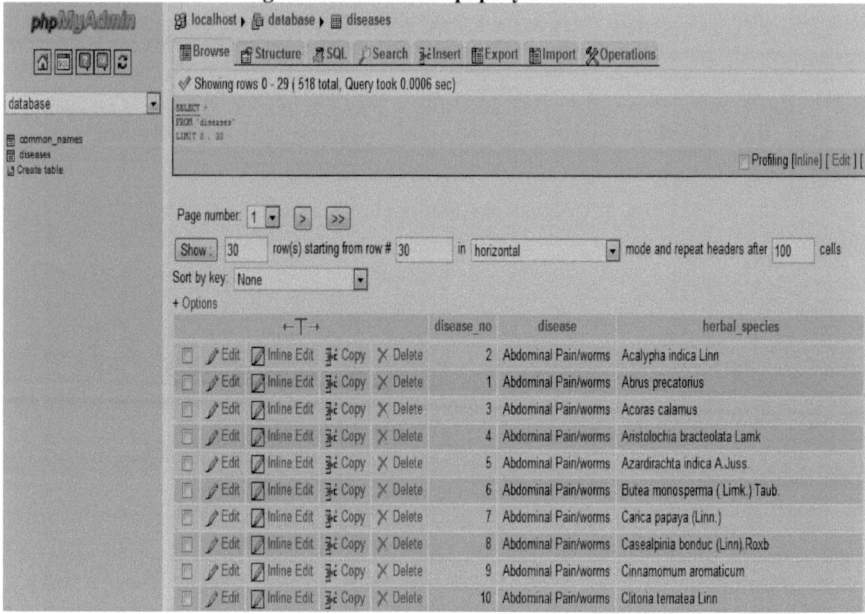

67 diseases and disorders were listed in the database along with their herbal species.

CHAPTER 4

RESULTS AND DISCUSSION

The outputs for the code are produced and are presented in below figures.

Fig 4: Main Page of the website (main.html)

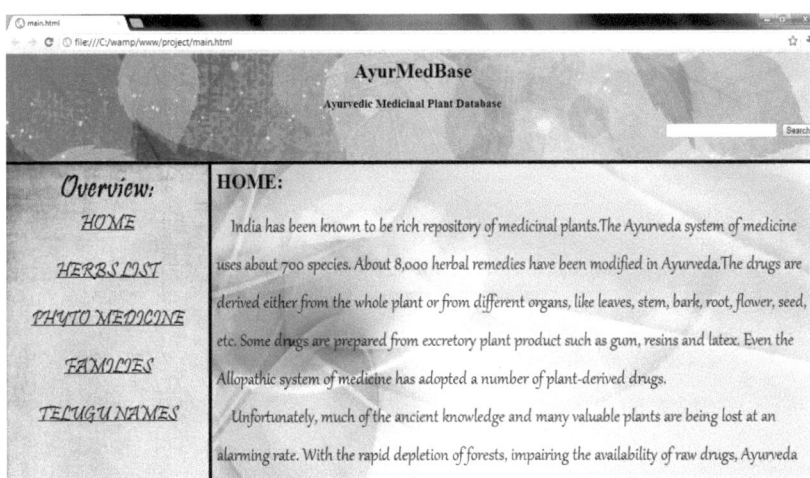

This is the main page of the portal where we can see 3 different frames. The left frame is a separate html

Fig 5: Search page (search.html)

Fig 6: Home page displayed in one of the frames in the main page (home.html)

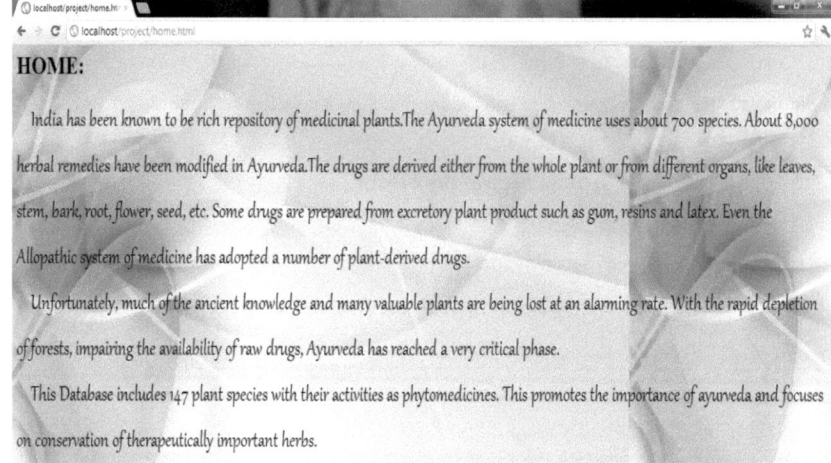

Fig 7: Page displaying different hyperlinks (links.html)

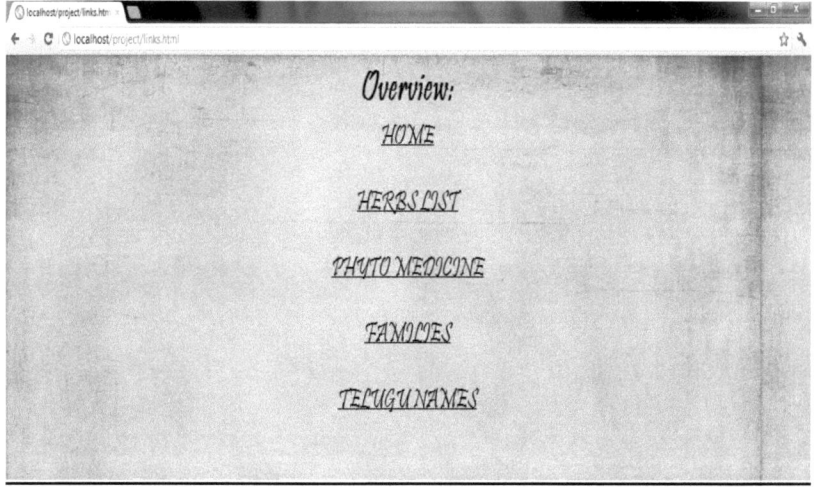

Fig 8: Monographs arranged in alphabetical order (alphabets.html)

Fig 9: Print screen displaying plant scientific names with the starting letter F (f.html)

Fig 10: Displaying alphabetical order- P (p.html)

Fig 11: Print screen displaying monograph (*Tagetes erecta.html*)
French Mary Gold

Botanical Name – *Tagetes erecta*
English –French Mary Gold
Hindi –Geynda
Telugu -Banthi chettu
Family –Asteraceae

Description:

This is a flowering plant with beautiful orange colored flowers. In villages and houses we come across this plant. During festival season we use these flowers in decoration purpose. Along with its beauty the plant is also important for its ayurvedic usage.

Uses:

1. Kajol prepared by using these flowers, ghee and camphor will stop burning sensation, itching, redness, water in eyes.
2. Flowers are grinded and juice is extracted. In the same way leaf decoction is also taken. These decoctions are much beneficial in the treatment of joint pains, head ache , tooth ache, ear pains.
3. For heart problems, use flower juice, leaf juice along with kandaki powder must be boiled and stored. Take this syrup for twice a day as 2 spoons per dose.
4. Jaundice patients must take leaf paste (2spoons) per day.
5. Leaf juice with sugar are useful in the treatment for urine disorders.
6. Leaf paste, pippal powder, pepper powder, dried ginger powder are mixed together in equal quantities and stored. This is useful in improving digestion.

Fig 12: displaying disease buttons linked with the medicinal plants (diseaselist.php)

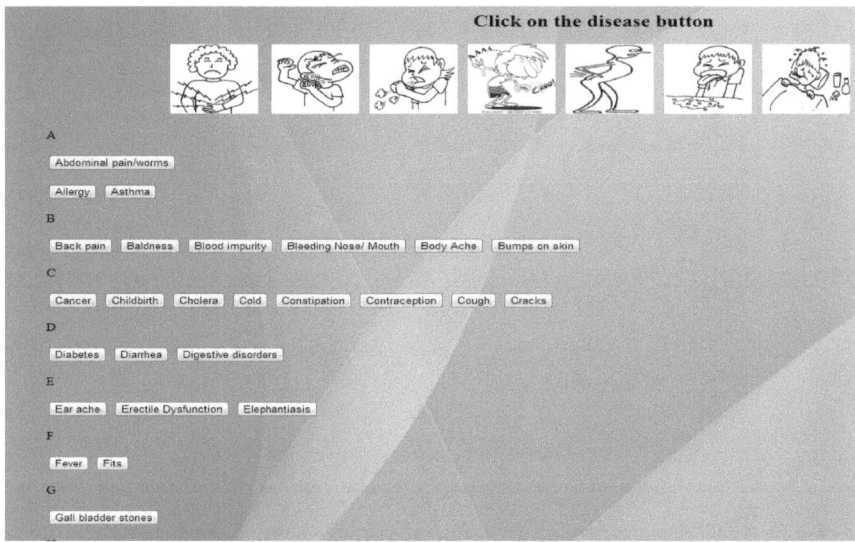

Fig 13: Disease button on click displays the medicinal plant hyperlinks (displaydisease.php)

DISEASE	HERBAL SPECIES
Abdominal Pain/worms	Acalypha indica Linn
Abdominal Pain/worms	Abrus precatorius
Abdominal Pain/worms	Acoras calamus
Abdominal Pain/worms	Aristolochia bracteolata Lamk
Abdominal Pain/worms	Azardirachta indica A.Juss.
Abdominal Pain/worms	Butea monosperma (Limk) Taub.
Abdominal Pain/worms	Carica papaya (Linn.)
Abdominal Pain/worms	Casealpinia bonduc (Linn) Roxb
Abdominal Pain/worms	Cinnamomum arcomaticum
Abdominal Pain/worms	Clitoria ternatea Linn
Abdominal Pain/worms	Cocos nucifera Linn

Fig 14: Family table (family.php)

LIST OF FAMILIES AND COMMON NAMES

SCIENTIFIC NAME	COMMON NAME	FAMILY
Acoras calamus	Sweet flag	Acoraceae
Achyranthus aspera Linn	Prickly flower	Amaranthaceae
Acalypha indica Linn	Indian acalypha	Euphorbiaceae
Acacia arabica wild.	Black babool, Indian Gum Arabic tree	Mimosaceae
Abrus precatorius	Indian Liquorice	Fabaceae
Abutilon indicum (Linn) sweet.	Country Mallow	Malvaceae
Adhatoda vasica nees.	Vasaka	Acanthaceae
Aegle marmelos (Linn.) Corr	Bael tree	Rutaceae
Aerva lanta (Linn) Juss	Javanese wood plant	Amaranthaceae
Alangium decapetalum	Sage Leaved, Alanghum	Alangiaceae
Allium cepa Linn.	Onion	Liliaceae

Fig 15: Table displaying telugu scientific and common names (teluguname.php)

LIST OF TELUGU NAMES AND COMMON NAMES

SCIENTIFIC NAMES	COMMON NAMES	TELUGU NAMES
Acoras calamus	Sweet flag	Vasa kommu, Vaja kommu
Achyranthus aspera Linn	Prickly flower	Uttareni
Acalypha indica Linn	Indian acalypha	Moorkonda, kuppinta
Acacia arabica wild.	Black babool, Indian Gum Arabic tree	Nalla tumma
Abrus precatorius	Indian Liquorice	Gurivinda theega , Guri ginja
Abutilon indicum (Linn) sweet.	Country Mallow	Duvvena chettu,Tuthari benda,Mudra benda
Adhatoda vasica nees.	Vasaka	Addasaram
Aegle marmelos (Linn.) Corr	Bael tree	Maredu
Aerva lanta (Linn) Juss	Javanese wood plant	konda pindi, telakapindi chettu
Alangium decapetalum	Sage Leaved, Alanghum	Uudugu chettu
Allium cepa Linn.	Onion	Neeruli

According to the book- Database on medicinal plants used in ayurveda belonging to Central Council for Research in Ayurveda & Siddha, authors mentioned about *Annona squamosa's* root as a powerful purgative. It is used in mental depression, spinal disorders and blood dysentery. The leaves are suppurative, stimulant, antispasmodic, sudrofic, anthelmentic, insecticidal and are useful in destroying lice. Bark is also an astringent and tonic [19].

"Plants for A Future" is a database which displays data about medicinal plants classified as Annuals, biennials, bulbs, climbers, perennials, shrubs and trees. The herb thyme has been shown to slow down the ageing process by maintaining the vigor of our body cells; sage is an excellent antiseptic for treating mouth ulcers and sore throats; camomile is a safe treatment for childrens' stomach upsets and garlic contains fungicides and is used in the treatment of Candida.

Prelude medicinal plants database belongs to metafro (Metafro Infosys is a catalogue of data sets and data sources related to Central Africa), they have assigned a card for each plant under the following headings: Name of plant, name of genus, bibliographical reference (with hyperlinks),country in which the sample was collected, vernacular name(s) of the plant, illness or symptom treated, frequency of use, type of medicine (human or veterinary), recipes for uses, i.e. the organs used, preparation of the drug, method of administration, the associated plants, any ritual accompanying the taking of the drug.

Raintree is a database dedicated to providing accurate and factual information on the important plants of the Amazon Rainforest, therefore this section of the Raintree web site is the most extensive. This database is authored and maintained by Dr. Leslie Taylor, ND. The individual plant database files are linked through various menus and pages to enable both professional readers and readers new to medicinal plants easy access to search the available plant information. Just click on one of the above tabs to navigate these pages. Each plant database file contains taxonomy data, phytochemical information, ethnobotanical data, uses in traditional medicine systems, and clinical research.

A research paper stated that more than half of the wild food plants have many edible parts, and more than two thirds of them have additional uses. Shoots, sprouting from the tips of plants, stems or roots, were the most widely cited as consumed regardless of the growth form or life cycle of the plant. Fruits were also common, particularly collected from trees and climbers. Wild food plants presented more than eleven additional uses, accentuating their overall relevance for rice farmers. The most common additional use is for medicine [20].

Dr. Duke's Phytochemical and Ethnobotanical Databases are classified into Chemicals and activities in a particular plant, High concentration chemicals, Chemicals with one activity, Ethnobotanical uses, List chemicals and activities for a plant. Here the genus or the common name of the plant can be given and its uses and Chemical(s) found in plant will be shown to be effective for the ailment medicated.

Tropicos was a database originally created for internal research but has since been made available to the world's scientific community. All of the nomenclatural, bibliographic, and specimen data accumulated in MBG's (Missouri botanical garden) electronic databases during the past 25 years are publicly available here. This system has over 1.2 million scientific names and 4.0 million specimen records.

A brief account with photographs of the `endangered / endemic` floral species of the Eastern Ghats region are listed by ENVIS – SDNP (partnership project at Centre on Eastern Ghats).

The following are few of the endangered plants found in Andhra Pradesh.

Plant name: Pterocarpus santalinus Linn.f.
Local/Vern. Name (s): Reds Sandalwood,
Rakta Chandan, Red Sanders Almug (E)
Family: Fabaceae
Red sandalwood is restricted to the southern parts of the Eastern Ghats.
Condition: Endangere

Plant name: Cycas beddomei Dyer.
Local/Vern. Names: Peritha, Pireetha
Family: Cycadaceae
Known only from the Cuddapah Hills in Andhra Pradesh State,
Condition: CR (Critically Endangered)

Plant name: Decalepis hamiltonii Wight & Arn.
Local/Vern. Name (s): Maredugeddalu, Nannari, Sariba, Svetasariva
Family: Asclepiadaceae

34

The species is endemic to Peninsular India, in forests of Andhra Pradesh.
Condition: Endangered

The present work on "AyurMedBase" contains a list of 147 plants. The main sql table displays the scientific name, common name, Telugu name and the family to which that particular plant belongs to. AyurMedBase is user friendly and its access is not restricted at any point. The keyword search is the best interface being run on the database.

To encourage the native knowledge on ayurveda and to preserve our traditional medicines, this database has been designed.

Ayurveda is an ancient system of natural & medical healing originated in India. Ayur means life and Veda means Science. Thus Ayurveda means science of life. It gives a total approach to health, healing and Longevity. The holistic system of medicine is supposed to be the oldest form of health care system available on planet today. It is believed that other healing systems were influenced by the knowledge of Ayurveda.

AyurMedBase is an attempt to record information on rich heritage of the medicinal plants in Andhra Pradesh. We gathered information on traditional, scientific therapeutics from local sources and literature, and compiled it into a comprehensive knowledge database, to make learners aware of availability of useful herbs around them, to familiarize learners with some common herbal plants and their uses and Utilization of available local herbal plants for the treatment of common ailments.

The characteristic feature of AyurMedBase is 'Disease Link', which displays each record and the list of plants. AyurMedBase can be accessed alphabetically using genus name for information on specific plants. These traditional plant medicines or herbal formulations might offer a natural key to unlock diabetic complications.

The database will be under constant development. It will be regularly updated based on availability of any new information.

CHAPTER 7

CONCLUSION

AyurMedBase is a medicinal plant database providing information and treatment of diseases. The database provides 147 plants information and their uses [21]. The common name, scientific name and other details with ayurvedic uses have been presented. This database is highly useful to people in the treatment and cure of diseases naturally from plants of Andhra Pradesh.

REFERENCES

[1] Ramar perumal Sam, Peter Natesan Pushparaj, Ponnampalam Gopalakrishnakone, "A compilation of bioactive compounds from Ayurveda ", J.Bioinformation, 2008, 3(3),100-110.

[2] P. P. Joy, J.Thomas,Samuel Mathew, Baby P. Skaria, "MEDICINAL PLANTS KERALA AGRICULTURAL UNIVERSITY",Aromatic and Medicinal Plants Research Station, J. Acta Pharmaceutica Sciencia, 1998,52, 89-100.

[3] Sukhdev Swami Handa, Suman Preet Singh Khanuja, Gennaro Longo, Dev Dutt Rakesh, "Extraction Technologies for Medicinal and Aromatic Plants",INTERNATIONAL CENTRE FOR SCIENCE AND HIGH TECHNOLOGY,Trieste,2008.

[4]Mudappa A, Oommen S. Amruth. "A database for medicinal plants used in treatment of asthma",J. Bioinformation,1998,2,10.

[5] Kiran SG, et al. Ind J Biotechnol. "A database for medicinal plants used in treatment of asthma",J. Bioinformation,2004,3,103.

[6] Padavala Ajay Babu ," A database of 389 medicinal plants for diabetes", J. Bioinformation. 2006, 1(4), 130–131.

[7] Mankil Jung, Moonsoo Park, Hyun Chul Lee, Yoon-Ho Kang, Eun Seok Kang, and Sang Ki Kim," Antidiabetic Agents from Medicinal Plants" J. Current Medicinal Chemistry, 2006, 13, 1203-1218.

[8] Nirmala Arulrayan Bioinformation.," A database for medicinal plants used in the treatment of diabetes and its secondary complications", J Bioinformation. 2007, 2(1), 22–23.

[9] Potshangbam Angamba Meetei, Pankaj Singh, Potshangbam Nongdam,N Prakash Prabhu, RS Rathore, and Vaibhav Vindal, "NeMedPlant: a database of therapeutic applications and

chemical constituents of medicinal plants from north-east region of India", Bioinformation. 2012, 8(4), 209–211.

[10] Akbar Masood and Mujtaba Shafi ," A database for medicinal and aromatic plants of JK (Jammu and Kashmir) in India", Bioinformation. 2005, 1(2), 56–57.

[11] Sarah E. J. Arnold1, Samia Faruq, Vincent Savolainen, Peter W. McOwan, Lars Chittka, "FReD: The Floral Reflectance Database — A Web Portal for Analyses of Flower Colour" J. Plos One, 2010

[12] Bhushan Patwardhan, Ashok D. B. Vaidya and Mukund Chorghade," Ayurveda and natural products drug discovery", CURRENT SCIENCE,MARCH 2004, vol. 86

[13] K.C. Dube, Aditya Kumar, Sanjay Dube," Personality Types in Ayurveda", The American Journal of Chinese Medicine (AJCM), 1983 ,Volume: 11, 25-34

[14] Rudolf Fritz Weiss, pdf on "Herbal Medicine"
[15] Jayajothi Elavarasu,T. Elavarasu, Mary Bowling, "HerbMed", J. MEDLINEPlus,2009

[16] Magali Lescot , Patrice Déhais, Gert Thijs, Kathleen Marchal, Yves Moreau,Yves Van de Peer1, Pierre Rouzé and Stephane Rombauts , "PlantCARE, a database of plant cis-acting regulatory elements and a portal to tools for in silico analysis of promoter sequences", J. Nucl. Acids Res. 2002, 30 (1),325-327.

[17] Dr. Elchuri Venkat Rao, "Andariki Ayurvedam- ayurveda jeevana vignanam".

[18] Dr. K. Nishteshwar, "Ayurveda vana moolika chikistsa".

[19] Kailash Chandra,B.G. Chaudhari,B.P.Dhar, G.V.R.Joseph, A.K.Mangal "Database on medicinal plants used in ayurveda", volume 8, Central Council for Research in Ayurveda & Siddha,2007

[20] Gisella S Cruz-Garcia and Lisa L Price," Ethnobotanical investigation of 'wild' food plants used by rice farmers in Kalasin, Northeast Thailand", Journal of Ethnobiology and Ethnomedicine 2011, 7(33).

[21] DSVGK Kaladhar, Traditional and Ayurvedic medicinal plants from India: Practices and Treatment for human diseases, Lambert Academic publishing,

WEB LINKS

http://ayurvedicmedicinalplants.com/

http://www.flowersofindia.in/index.html

http://www.medicinalplants.in/v/index.php/aboutfrlhtdb

http://www.pharmabiz.com/NewsDetails.aspx?aid=66750&sid=1

http://www.herbsnspicesinfo.com/

http://www.botanical.com/botanical/mgmh/comindxa.html

http://oregonstate.edu/dept/ldplants/

http://woodyplants.nres.uiuc.edu/

http://www.ncbi.nlm.nih.gov/pubmed/

http://www.plosone.org/home.action

http://www.ncbi.nlm.nih.gov/mesh

http://www.pfaf.org/user/medicinaluses.aspx

http://www.metafro.be/prelude/plant_collection

http://www.rain-tree.com/plants.htm

http://www.tropicos.org/Home.aspx

http://envis-eptri.ap.nic.in/images/SDNPFirstReport.pdf